A+ books

Bilingual Picture Dictionaries

My First Book of
Mandarin Chinese Words

apple
苹果
(píngguǒ)

by Katy R. Kudela

Translator: Translations.com

Capstone press

Mankato, Minnesota

Table of Contents

How to Use This Dictionary

This book is full of useful words in both Mandarin and English. The English word appears first, followed by the Mandarin word. Look below each Mandarin word for help to sound it out. Try reading the words aloud.

Topic Heading in English

Topic Heading in Mandarin

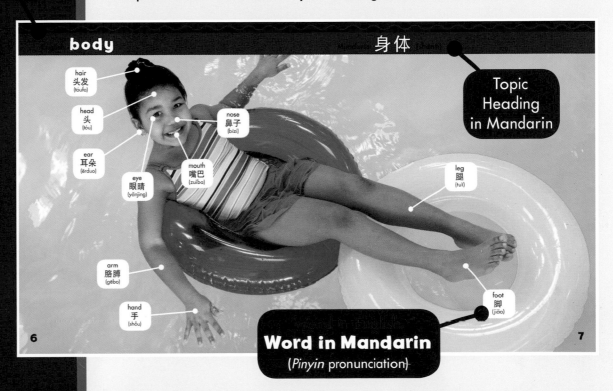

body 身体

- hair 头发 (tóufa)
- head 头 (tóu)
- nose 鼻子 (bízi)
- ear 耳朵 (ěrduo)
- eye 眼睛 (yǎnjing)
- mouth 嘴巴 (zuǐba)
- leg 腿 (tuǐ)
- arm 胳膊 (gēbo)
- hand 手 (shǒu)
- foot 脚 (jiǎo)

6   7

Word in Mandarin
(*Pinyin* pronunciation)

Notes about the Mandarin Chinese Language

Pinyin is a system of writing Chinese that spells out the sounds of the words using Roman letters. Most of the *Pinyin* pronunciations can be read like English. A few letters have different sounds. Below are some additional pronunciations to help.

q (ch)	**z** (dz)	**e** (uh)	**ui** (way)
x (sh)	**zh** (dge)	**u** (oo)	**ü** (eu)

Pinyin also uses four tones. These tones mean that vowel sounds can be said in different ways.

ā, ē, ī, ō, ū = high-level tone, slightly higher than regular speech
á, é, í, ó, ú = rising tone, sound rises like when asking a question
ǎ, ě, ǐ, ǒ, ǔ = dipping tone, sound falls and then rises
à, è, ì, ò, ù = falling tone, starts high and then falls

English:

uncle
叔叔
(shūshu)

mother
妈妈
(māma)

cousin
表兄弟
(biǎoxiōngdì)

aunt
阿姨
(āyí)

baby
宝宝
(bǎo bǎo)

4

家庭

grandmother
祖母
(zǔmǔ)

father
爸爸
(bàba)

grandfather
祖父
(zǔfù)

brother
兄弟
(xiōngdì)

sister
姐妹
(jiěmèi)

hair
头发
(tóufa)

head
头
(tóu)

nose
鼻子
(bízi)

ear
耳朵
(ěrduo)

mouth
嘴巴
(zuǐba)

eye
眼睛
(yǎnjing)

arm
胳膊
(gēbo)

hand
手
(shǒu)

leg
腿
(tuǐ)

foot
脚
(jiǎo)

7

pajamas
睡衣
(shuìyī)

coat
外套
(wàitào)

shorts
短裤
(duǎn kù)

boot
靴子
(xuēzi)

8

shoe
鞋
(xié)

hat
帽子
(màozi)

pants
裤子
(kùzi)

sock
袜子
(wàzi)

shirt
衬衫
(chènshān)

dress
连衣裙
(liányīqún)

kite
风筝
(fēngzheng)

doll
洋娃娃
(yángwáwa)

puzzle
拼图
(pīntú)

train
火车
(huǒchē)

wagon
推车
(tuīchē)

玩具

puppet
木偶
(mù'ǒu)

skateboard
滑板
(huábǎn)

jump rope
跳绳
(tiào shéng)

ball
球
(qiú)

bat
球棒
(qiú bàng)

window
窗
(chuāng)

picture
图画
(túhuà)

lamp
灯
(dēng)

dresser
梳妆台
(shūzhuāngtái)

curtain
窗帘
(chuānglián)

blanket
毯子
(tǎnzi)

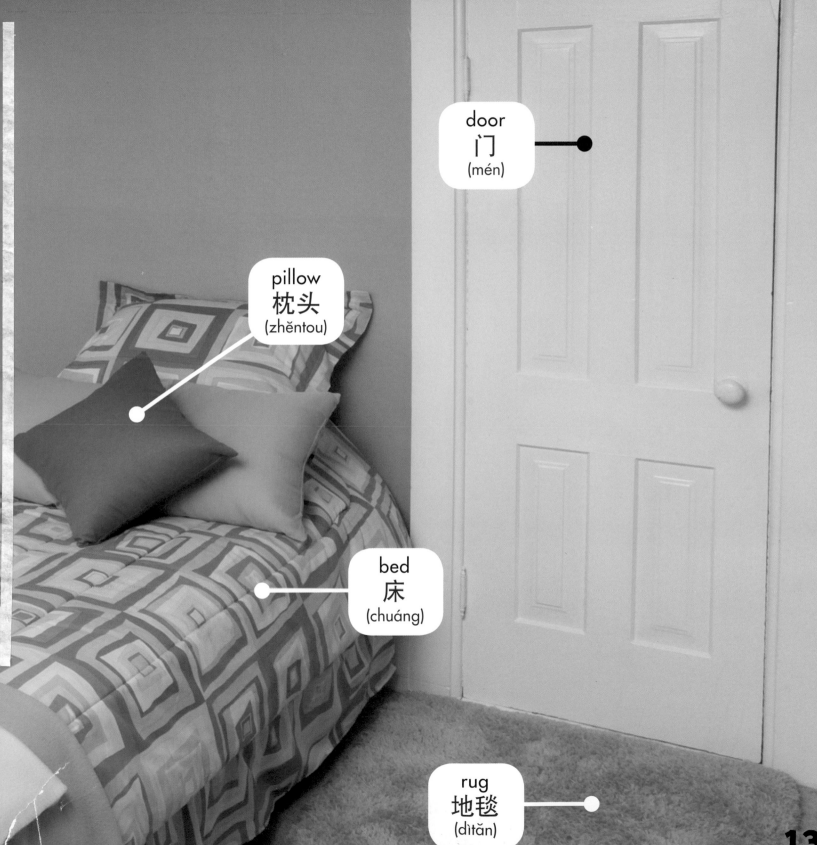

door
门
(mén)

pillow
枕头
(zhěntou)

bed
床
(chuáng)

rug
地毯
(dìtǎn)

bathtub
浴缸
(yùgāng)

soap
肥皂
(féizào)

toilet
马桶
(mǎtǒng)

14

卫生间

mirror
镜子
(jìngzi)

toothbrush
牙刷
(yáshuā)

toothpaste
牙膏
(yágāo)

sink
水池
(shuǐchí)

comb
梳子
(shūzi)

towel
毛巾
(máojīn)

brush
刷子
(shuāzi)

15

bowl
碗
(wǎn)

stove
炉子
(lúzi)

pot
锅
(guō)

oven
烤箱
(kǎoxiāng)

厨房

refrigerator
冰箱
(bīngxiāng)

knife
刀
(dāo)

spoon
勺
(sháo)

plate
盘子
(pánzi)

table
桌子
(zhuōzi)

fork
叉
(chā)

milk
牛奶
(niúnǎi)

carrot
胡萝卜
(húluó-bo)

bread
面包
(miànbāo)

apple
苹果
(píngguǒ)

butter
黄油
(huángyóu)

18

egg
鸡蛋
(jīdàn)

pea
豌豆
(wāndòu)

orange
桔子
(júzi)

sandwich
三明治
(sānmíngzhì)

rice
大米
(dàmǐ)

19

farm

tractor
拖拉机
(tuōlājī)

hay
干草
(gāncǎo)

fence
栅栏
(zhàlán)

farmer
农民
(nóngmín)

sheep
羊
(yáng)

pig
猪
(zhū)

horse
马
(mǎ)

barn
粮仓
(liángcāng)

cow
牛
(niú)

chicken
鸡
(jī)

21

leaf
叶子
(yèzi)

butterfly
蝴蝶
(húdié)

flower
花
(huā)

shovel
铲子
(chǎnzi)

bird
鸟
(niǎo)

worm
虫
(chóng)

plant
植物
(zhíwù)

grass
草
(cǎo)

dirt
泥土
(nítǔ)

seed
种子
(zhǒngzi)

Edamame Green Soybean
Tohya

Glycine max

$2.99
Net Weight
15 grams

80 days
Warm season
crop - plant after
last chance of
spring frost

So high in
protein, it is
called "the meat
without bones."
Boiled, beans
are popped out
of the pod into
your mouth for
a culinary
delight!

23

brown
棕色
(zōngsè)

purple
紫色
(zǐsè)

orange
橙色
(chéngsè)

white
白色
(báisè)

red
红色
(hóngsè)

black
黑色
(hēisè)

24

颜色 (yánsè)

pink
粉色
(fěnsè)

blue
蓝色
(lánsè)

yellow
黄色
(huángsè)

green
绿色
(lǜsè)

teacher
老师
(lǎoshī)

book
书
(shū)

crayon
蜡笔
(làbǐ)

desk
书桌
(shūzhuō)

pencil
铅笔
(qiānbǐ)

clock
挂钟
(guàzhōng)

map
地图
(dìtú)

computer
电脑
(diànnǎo)

chair
椅子
(yǐzi)

paper
纸
(zhǐ)

traffic light
红绿灯
(hónglǜdēng)

library
图书馆
(túshūguǎn)

store
商店
(shāngdiàn)

LIBRARY

ONE WAY →

Tuesday 2:00-5:00
Thursday 2:00-6:00

bicycle
自行车
(zìxíngchē)

car
汽车
(qìchē)

28

城市

tree
树
(shù)

bus
公共汽车
(gōnggòng qìchē)

park
公园
(gōngyuán)

street
街道
(jiēdào)

sign
标志
(biāozhì)

STOP

Numbers • 数字 (shùzì)

1. one • 一 (yī)
2. two • 二 (èr)
3. three • 三 (sān)
4. four • 四 (sì)
5. five • 五 (wǔ)
6. six • 六 (liù)
7. seven • 七 (qī)
8. eight • 八 (bā)
9. nine • 九 (jiǔ)
10. ten • 十 (shí)

Useful Phrases • 常用短语 (chángyòng duǎnyǔ)

yes • 是 (shì)

no • 不是 (bù shì)

hello • 你好 (nǐ hǎo)

good-bye • 再见 (zài jiàn)

good morning • 早上好 (zǎoshang hǎo)

good night • 晚安 (wǎnān)

please • 请 (qǐng)

thank you • 谢谢 (xièxie)

excuse me • 对不起 (duìbuqǐ)

My name is _____. • 我的名字是 _____. (wǒ de míngzi shì)

Read More

Amery, Heather. *First Hundred Words in Chinese.* London: Usborne Books, 2009.

Greenwood, Elinor. *Get Talking Chinese: Mandarin Chinese for Beginners.* DK Get Talking. New York: Dorling Kindersley, 2007.

Mandarin Chinese Picture Dictionary. Princeton, N.J.: Berlitz, 2008.

Internet Sites

FactHound offers a safe, fun way to find Internet sites related to this book. All of the sites on FactHound have been researched by our staff.

Here's all you do:

Visit *www.facthound.com*

FactHound will fetch the best sites for you!

A+ Books are published by Capstone Press,
151 Good Counsel Drive, P.O. Box 669, Mankato, Minnesota 56002.
www.capstonepub.com

 Books published by Capstone Press are manufactured with paper
containing at least 10 percent post-consumer waste.

Library of Congress Cataloging-in-Publication Data
Kudela, Katy R.
    My first book of Mandarin Chinese words / by Katy R. Kudela.
    p. cm. — (A+ books. Bilingual picture dictionaries)
    Summary: "Simple text paired with themed photos invite the reader to learn to speak
Mandarin Chinese" — Provided by publisher.
    Includes bibliographical references.
    ISBN 978-1-4296-3297-3 (library binding)
    ISBN 978-1-4296-4371-9 (paperback)
    1. Picture dictionaries, Chinese — Juvenile literature. 2. Picture dictionaries,
English — Juvenile literature. 3. Chinese language — Dictionaries, Juvenile — English.
4. English language — Dictionaries, Juvenile — Chinese. I. Title. II. Series.
PL1423.K83 2010
495.1'321 — dc22   2009005517

Credits

Juliette Peters, designer; Wanda Winch, media researcher

Photo Credits

Capstone Press/Gary Sundermeyer, cover (pig), 20 (farmer with tractor, pig)
Capstone Press/Karon Dubke, cover (ball, sock), back cover (toothbrush, apple), 1, 3,
    4–5, 6–7, 8–9, 10–11, 12–13, 14–15, 16–17, 18–19, 22–23, 24–25, 26–27
Image Farm, back cover, 1, 2, 31, 32 (design elements)
iStockphoto/Andrew Gentry, 28 (main street)
Photodisc, cover (flower)
Shutterstock/Adrian Matthiassen, cover (butterfly); David Hughes, 20 (hay); Eric Isselee,
    20–21 (horse); hamurishi, 28 (bike); Jim Mills, 29 (stop sign); Kelli Westfal, 28
    (traffic light); Levgeniia Tikhonova, 21 (chickens); Margo Harrison, 20 (sheep);
    MaxPhoto, 21 (cow and calf); Melinda Fawver, 29 (bus); Robert Elias, 20–21
    (barn, fence); Vladimir Mucibabic, 28–29 (city skyline)

Note to Parents, Teachers, and Librarians

Learning to speak a second language at a young age has been shown to improve overall
academic performance, boost problem-solving ability, and foster an appreciation for other
cultures. Early exposure to language skills provides a strong foundation for other subject
areas, including math and reasoning. Introducing children to a second language can help to
lay the groundwork for future academic success and cultural awareness.